THE RETURN OF THE
BALD EAGLE

HEATHER MOORE NIVER

PowerKiDS
press.

New York

Published in 2018 by The Rosen Publishing Group, Inc.
29 East 21st Street, New York, NY 10010

First Edition

Editor: Theresa Morlock
Book Design: Reann Nye

Photo Credits: Cover Stan Tekiela Author/Naturalist/Wildlife Photographer/Moment/Getty Images; p. 4 Richard Lowthian/Shutterstock.com; p. 5 (Pyrenean ibex) dragoms/Moment Open/Getty Images; p. 5 (jaguar) Travel Stock/Shutterstock.com; p. 5 (Arctic fox, hippopotamus) bikeriderlondon/Shutterstock.com; pp. 5 (orangutan), 7 Sergey Uryadnikov/Shutterstock.com; p. 5 (Wyoming toad) https://commons.wikimedia.org/wiki/File:Bufo_baxteri-3.jpg; p. 7 Sergey Uryadnikov/Shutterstock.com; p. 8 Menno Schaefer/Shutterstock.com; p. 9 Ray Hennessy/Shutterstock.com; p. 10 W. Perry Conway/Corbis/Getty Images; p. 11 Mike R Turner/Moment Open/Getty Images; p. 12 Jeff Foott/Discovery Channel Images/Getty Images; p. 13 Paul Nicklen/National Geographic/Getty Images; p. 15 DMS Foto/Shutterstock.com; p. 16 Alfred Eisenstaedt/The LIFE Picture Collection/Getty Images; p. 17 Wilfred Marissen/Shutterstock.com; p. 18 nomad-photo.eu/Shutterstock.com; p. 19 Merrimon Crawford/Shutterstock.com; pp. 21, 29 Brian E Kushner/Shutterstock.com; p. 22 Martin Prochazkacz/Shutterstock.com; p. 23 Don Pitcher/Design Pics/First Light/Getty Images; p. 24 Stephen Osman/Los Angeles Times/Getty Images; p. 25 Martin Michael Rudlof/Shutterstock.com; p. 27 Brian Guzzetti/First Light/Getty Images; p. 28 Anatoliy Lukich/Shutterstock.com; p. 30 Riegsecker/Shutterstock.com.

Cataloging-in-Publication Data

Names: Niver, Heather Moore.
Title: The return of the bald eagle / Heather Moore Niver.
Description: New York : PowerKids Press, 2018. | Series: Bouncing back from extinction | Includes index.
Identifiers: ISBN 9781508156260 (pbk.) | ISBN 9781508156192 (library bound) | ISBN 9781508156079 (6 pack)
Subjects: LCSH: Bald eagle–Juvenile literature.
Classification: LCC QL696.F32 N58 2018 | DDC 598.9'42–dc23

Manufactured in the United States of America

CPSIA Compliance Information: Batch #BS17PK: For Further Information contact Rosen Publishing, New York, New York at 1-800-237-9932

CONTENTS

A SOARING SUCCESS!

During the 1700s, bald eagles soared across North America. There may have been as many as 100,000 nesting eagles in the United States alone. Over the years, however, eagle populations have suffered as a result of human activities. People have hunted them, destroyed their **habitats**, and poisoned them. By 1963, there were fewer than 1,000 bald eagles in the lower 48 United States.

Thankfully, beginning in the 1970s, the U.S. Fish and Wildlife Service put the bald eagle under legal protection. Today almost 10,000 nesting pairs of bald eagles live throughout the lower United States. Studying the bald eagle's history helps us understand the challenges that endangered animals face and how we may improve their chances for survival. The bald eagle's progress is an exciting success story for endangered animals.

Although the **species** teetered on the edge of extinction, bald eagle populations are finally on the rise again.

CONSERVATION STATUS CHART

EXTINCT

Having no living members.

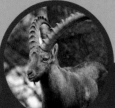

Pyrenean ibex

EXTINCT IN THE WILD

Living members only in captivity.

Wyoming toad

CRITICALLY ENDANGERED

At highest risk of becoming extinct.

Sumatran orangutan

ENDANGERED VULNERABLE

High risk of extinction in the wild.

hippopotamus

NEAR THREATENED

Likely to become endangered soon.

jaguar

LEAST CONCERN

Lowest risk of endangerment.

Arctic fox

5

THE RISE OF A REGAL RAPTOR

The bald eagle became the symbol of the United States in 1782 when it was used on the Great Seal of the United States. The eagle was selected because of its beauty, strength, and long life. Although it achieved fame as the national bird of America, the bald eagle's status didn't help keep this beautiful bird safe.

Bald eagles have few predators. Very young eagles are at risk from larger birds of prey and mammals such as bears and foxes. For the most part, however, adult eagles have only one predator to fear: humans. People have had a shockingly negative effect on bald eagles. Their actions have harmed this bold bird in many ways.

A BIG BIRD!

A bald eagle's body is about 34 to 43 inches (86.4 to 109.2 cm) long. Its wingspan is 6 to 8 feet (1.8 to 2.4 m). This **raptor** weighs about 6.5 to 14 pounds (3 to 6.5 kg). Male bald eagles tend to be a little bit smaller than females. In the wild, bald eagles can live for 20 to 30 years.

The bald eagle is the only eagle that lives solely in North America.

Some settlers saw the bald eagle as competition for fish and other game and a danger to their livestock. Bald eagles were often hunted, trapped, and poisoned. People also cleared the land on which the bald eagles lived and hunted. Eagles avoid areas with lots of people, so as human populations grew, the bald eagles left their home ranges.

By 1940, the bald eagle population was dangerously low. The U.S. government realized this

WHO CARES ABOUT EXTINCTION?

The extinction of a predator like the bald eagle might create an extinction pattern. For example, when the extinct animal is no longer around to eat its prey, the prey's population may increase. The prey may eat all the food in an area, leaving none for other animals. Those animals may then go extinct. This is a common pattern when one animal goes extinct.

Between 1917 and 1952, at least 128,000 eagles in Alaska were killed by paid hunters. It's possible that more than 150,000 were actually killed.

national symbol needed protection right away. The Bald Eagle Protection Act was passed to protect the birds themselves as well as their feathers, eggs, and nests. Unfortunately, this act was loosely **enforced** at first. Incidents still occurred, including one in which more than 750 eagles were killed on one farm.

THE BALD EAGLE'S DIET

Bald eagles are big birds that require plenty of food to fuel their bodies. Fish are one of their favorite dishes. Their sharp beaks are perfect for tearing meat into small pieces. Eagle feet have **talons**, which are great for grabbing fish out of the water. They have strong leg muscles to help them do this.

Bald eagle feet have bumps called "spicules," which help the birds keep hold of slippery fish.

When fish are unavailable, bald eagles are willing to mix up their menu. Sometimes they eat smaller birds such as ducks, or small mammals such as rabbits, squirrels, prairie dogs, and muskrats. Sometimes bald eagles eat **carrion**. Bald eagles often steal carrion from ospreys, which are another type of raptor. When an osprey returns to its nest with prey, the waiting eagle pesters the osprey until it drops its meal. Then the eagle swoops in to steal it.

Bald eagles live in habitats where there are lots of animals to hunt. They usually live near bodies of water, such as lakes, rivers, and the sea. Bald eagles like areas where they can **roost** and build large nests up high. They also prefer to live away from human activity.

When Europeans arrived in North America, the bald eagle population was large. But as the human population grew and people moved westward, they began to destroy eagle habitats. They cleared the forests where eagles hunted for food. Without places to hunt, some bald eagles died of starvation. Without places to nest,

BALD EAGLE FAMILIES

Bald eagle pairs stay together for life. The male and female eagles work together to build a nest for their young. Nest building can take between one and three months. Mother eagles lay about three eggs per year. They sit on the eggs for a little over a month while the young develop inside. The eaglets leave the nest after 10 to 14 weeks.

Bald eagles need strong trees for their nests, which can be up to about 10 feet (3 m) across. These heavy nests can weigh more than 1,000 pounds (453.6 kg)! The biggest on record was 20 feet (6 m) tall.

adult eagles had fewer baby eagles. Humans also hunted and fished for the same animals eagles ate, leaving less for these hungry birds.

THE HUNTER IS HUNTED

Eagle feathers are important objects in many Native American cultures. Although some Native American peoples did hunt bald eagles, the eagle population wasn't in danger until Europeans arrived in North America.

For many years, the bald eagle was hunted for a number of reasons. People hunted eagles for sport or for the challenge of killing such a big, beautiful bird. Other hunters felt that this predator caused problems in places where they liked to fish.

People hunted bald eagles in an effort to limit the competition for valuable fish, such as salmon, and other wild animals. However, studies later showed that bald eagles were not hurting the salmon population too much with their hunting. The fishermen could still catch plenty of salmon to sell or to eat.

Anyone who kills a bald eagle may be punished by up to two years in prison.

CURBING CHEMICALS

In spite of the Bald Eagle Protection Act of 1940, bald eagle numbers continued to fall over the next few decades. From the 1940s through the 1960s, many farmers used a **pesticide** known as DDT to kill insects that damaged their crops. People also used DDT to kill mosquitos. Rodents ate the poison-covered plants, and bald eagles ate the rodents. Bald eagles then **absorbed**

RACHEL CARSON'S SILENT SPRING

In 1962, a biologist named Rachel Carson wrote *Silent Spring*. In this book, she described the dangers of pesticides such as DDT and their damage to wildlife and the environment. Her writing brought attention to the issue of pollution. People began to think about the larger effects pesticides had on the environment.

Bald eagles build their nests at the tops of trees using sticks and twigs. They lay about two to three eggs at a time.

DDT into their bodies. It also washed into the rivers and other waters where eagles caught fish.

Eagles that had a lot of DDT in their bodies laid eggs with weak shells. Often, the eggshells broke before the babies were ready to hatch. The eaglets were not ready to survive. The eggs could be crushed easily because of the thin shells. DDT also might have prevented some bald eagles from laying eggs at all.

POISONED

Lead also caused many bald eagle deaths. Lead is a metal that is extremely poisonous when eaten. It can make animals extremely ill or even kill them. Sometimes hunters shoot animals such as deer and ducks with bullets made of lead. Some of the animals get away from the hunter and die in the wild.

copper bullets

Lead bullets are now illegal in California. Other states have put laws into place that limit the use of lead. Unfortunately, this issue is still unresolved.

Bald eagles sometimes eat the carrion, lead and all, or eat other animals that have eaten carrion containing lead. Because young bald eagles are still learning their hunting skills, they are more likely to take advantage of an easier meal. Unfortunately, that puts them at a higher risk for lead poisoning. Using bullets made of copper or tin could help solve this problem and keep both animals and the people who hunt them safe.

In 1972, the Environmental Protection Agency (EPA) officially banned DDT. The Endangered Species Preservation Act of 1966 protected the areas where bald eagles fed, built nests, and roosted. It was now illegal to disturb these areas. After people discovered the damage caused by DDT, the government passed more laws to protect bald eagles.

After the U.S. government passed the Endangered Species Act of 1973, the bald eagle was added to the endangered species list in 1978. It was listed as endangered in most of the lower 48 states but considered threatened in Michigan, Minnesota, Oregon, Washington, and Wisconsin. Bald eagles were not listed as threatened or endangered in Alaska or Hawaii. Alaska's bald eagle population remained strong, and these birds don't live in Hawaii.

The Bald Eagle Protection Act of 1940 was revised in 1972 to make punishments for illegal hunting more severe.

BRINGING BACK THE BIRDS

Slowly but surely, the bald eagle population grew again. On June 28, 2007, they were removed from the threatened and endangered lists. However, they still need our protection. The Bald and Golden Eagle Protection Act is still enforced. This law makes it illegal to shoot, poison, or otherwise hurt bald and golden eagles. It's also illegal to own, buy, sell, trade, or transport them. The law protects every part of their bodies—including feathers—as well as

Eagles **migrate** south where more food is available to hunt during the winter. They usually migrate in groups, averaging speeds up to 30 miles (48 km) per hour.

their nests and eggs. People can't hunt or own eagles without a **permit**. If they do and they are caught, they must pay a fine, go to jail, or both.

Bald eagles are also protected under the Migratory Bird Treaty Act. Birds that migrate over international borders are covered under this law.

Another way to protect bald eagles and increase their population is called hacking. In eagle hacking, young eagles are kept at an artificial nest on a high tower in an area where there aren't many bald eagles. Later, they are released into the wild from that tower. Young eagles are known to return to the area where they were raised, so many of the bald eagles came back to live in the area near the tower. They raise their babies there, too.

In eagle hacking, it's important for people to keep their distance from young eagles. Becoming too comfortable with people can be dangerous for eagles.

The American Eagle Foundation was created in Tennessee in 1985. Al Cecere of Nashville, Tennessee, formed the foundation in response to a photo showing 23 bald eagles that had been killed by hunters. With the help of the Dollywood Company, the foundation built the United States Eagle Center in Pigeon Forge, Tennessee. The center is dedicated to breeding and caring for bald eagles and teaching the public about them.

The American Eagle Foundation hacked and released 145 bald eagles and 12 golden eagles in Tennessee's Great Smoky Mountains between 1992 and 2015. The San Francisco Zoo has the largest bald eagle breeding and release program in the country. Zoo employees have released 95 eagles since 1991.

CHALLENGES

Bald eagle populations continue to grow, but they are not out of danger quite yet. In March 2016, a number of bald eagles were found dead in Washington, D.C., and Maryland. Experts are still trying to figure out what caused so many of these birds to die.

Although DDT is banned for most uses, scientists still find evidence of it when they test eagles and their eggs. They also find lead, mercury, and **PCBs**.

Other types of pollution are a problem for bald eagles, too. For example, an oil spill in 1989 in Prince William Sound, Alaska, took the lives of many animals, including about 250 bald eagles. Another 4 percent of the local eagle population died the following year. It took until 1995 before the eagle population returned to normal numbers.

Mercury, a chemical element, can prevent bald eagle eggs from hatching.

A BRIGHTER FUTURE

Do you want to help the bald eagle population? You might see a nest when you're hiking or camping. It's exciting to see a bald eagle in real life, but try to stay as far away as you can. Also, keep away from their winter roosting areas. You can help protect their populations by giving them a safe space in which to live. Eagles might leave their nests if humans disturb them.

If we continue to be aware of how our actions affect wildlife such as bald eagles, their populations should continue to be healthy.

The progress made toward saving the bald eagle from extinction is exciting and hopeful. If people continue to make sure their actions do not harm bald eagles, the number of eagles should continue to increase, which is a promising beginning for a brighter future.

THE HISTORY OF THE BALD EAGLE

June 20, 1782 — The bald eagle is chosen for the great seal of the United States.

The Bald Eagle Protection Act is passed. It is now illegal to kill bald eagles in the United States. — **1940**

1962 — The Bald Eagle Protection Act is changed to include golden eagles and renamed the Bald and Golden Eagle Protection Act.

Only 417 pairs of bald eagles remain in North America. — **1963**

1967 — Bald eagles are listed as protected under the Endangered Species Preservation Act.

DDT, which killed many bald eagles or damaged their eggs, is banned. — **1972**

1978 — Bald eagles are listed as threatened and endangered species under the Endangered Species Act.

An oil spill from the *Exxon Valdez* ship in Alaska's Prince William Sound kills about 250 bald eagles. The local population of eagles decreased by another 4 percent the following year. — **1989**

1995 — The U.S. Fish and Wildlife Service (USFWS) lists bald eagles as threatened rather than endangered.

The USFWS removed bald eagles from the endangered species list. It estimates 9,789 nesting pairs live in the lower United States. — **2007**

GLOSSARY

absorb: To take in and hold onto something.

carrion: A dead, rotting animal.

enforce: To give force to something, such as a law.

habitat: The natural home for plants, animals, and other living things.

migrate: Move from one place to another for feeding or having babies.

PCB: Any of the toxic chemical compounds called "polychlorinated biphenyls."

permit: A printed document from a government or organization that allows someone to own or do something.

pesticide: Something used to kill pests such as bugs.

raptor: A bird that hunts for food. Also called a bird of prey.

roost: To settle down for rest or sleep.

species: A group of plants or animals that are all the same kind.

talons: A bird's sharp claws.

INDEX

WEBSITES

Due to the changing nature of Internet links, PowerKids Press has developed an online list of websites related to the subject of this book. This site is updated regularly. Please use this link to access the list: www.powerkidslinks.com/bbe/eagle